The localization of Atlantis encoded by the Pyramids of Egypt and the Great Sphinx

A Discovery of Dr. Michael Hoffmann made
at 16.04.2018

described here in this little book.

Perhaps you feel bored while reading the
following pages, or you find hair in the
soup, or something did not please of my
derivation ... to anticipate at the very
beginning:

I do not care about that.

And please note: I am not in court here.
What is described here in this little book is
my personal oppinion only. Dankeschön.

The localization of Atlantis encoded by the Pyramids of Egypt and the Great Sphinx

10.000 years ago, worldwide sea level due to the ice age was about 120 meters lower than today, because most of the water was fixed as solid ice.

These old coastal courses are visible on satellite pictures from google maps as light blue areas (**Fig.1**).

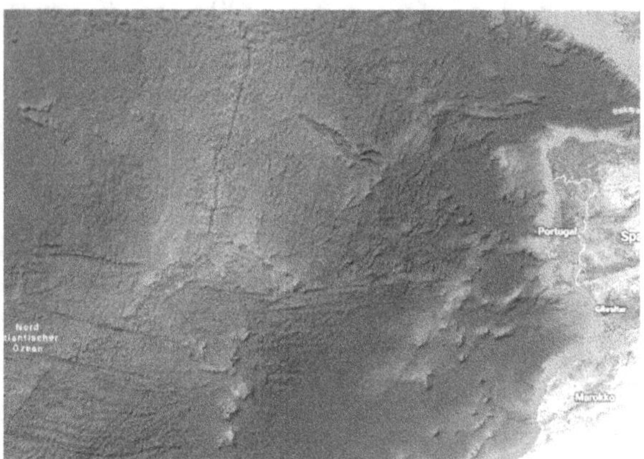

Fig.1: Ancient coastal courses are recognized as light blue (light gray) areas. Also, archipelagos can be identified.

In the northern atlantic ocean, there are numerous areas, that did not need to have been under water at that time. Possibly, these are areas that formed archipelagos and also appear to be light blue (light gray).

Particularly striking in this consideration is a small area located just south of the Azores at degree of latitide 29°58′ N.

This area is striking because a probably former island can easily trace an equilateral triangle (**Fig.2**).

The Probability that such an object is of natural origin is close to zero for three exactly straight lines that form a geometric figure.

Such objects can only have been created by humans. In addition, the surface of this object is obviously absolutely even.

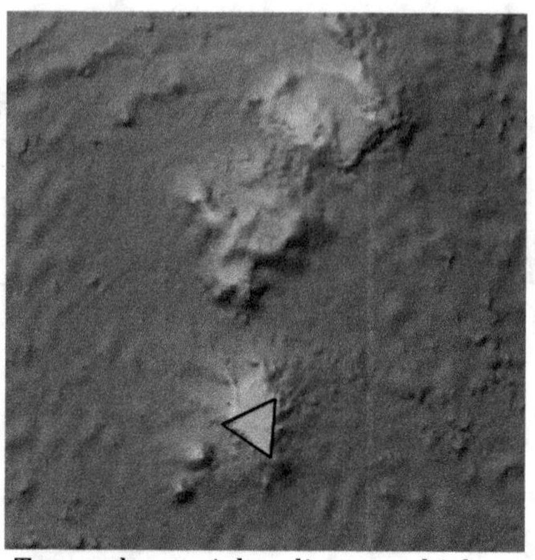

Fig.2: Tapered straight lines, which can be combined to form a triangle, equilateral.

In this area, to the east, there are numerous parallel abd also differently ordered lines, as well as regular elevations, which evidently move away from a centre.

However, the most striking aspect of this area is the overall circular arrangement, or the slight possibility of suggestively drawing a circle (**Fig.3**).

In the exact centre of this circle is an elevation, which is of such a strange shape, that it must be constructed as well.

In the northeastern region of this area there is another circular construction, but smaller.

Thus, in this area a total of at least three geometric patterns are present. Thereby, the probability of a natural event, for example an impact crater, or suggestive imagination is possibly very low.

If you look closely at Figure 2 you can also note a semicircle left to the triangle.

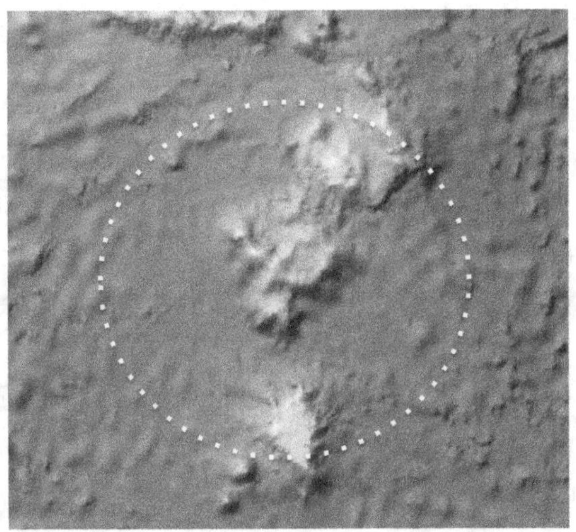

Fig.3: Geometric patterns (circles, triangle, lines) on the ground of the atlantic ocean.

In any case, this outer circle has a huge diameter of about 299 kilometers. This corresponds to an ancient Egyptian unit of length, 1000 foot (called Djeser).

This big circle could be an impact crater, however that does not explain the structures in the inside.

Particularly, in the centre of the circle is that thing that looks more like it was created. It somehow resembles a sign unknown to me. However I am sure it is a sign that exists or had exist elsewhere.

Thus, the big cirlce could have been a dike, because most of this area was below sea level at that time.

So far, this would already be a basis for one or the other: Yes, there could be something that has actually been constructed by humans.

And that must have happened before the sea level has risen, which is about 9000 before Christ.

But there is more:

For this we venture a jump from this area far to the east, to Giza in Egypt (**Fig.4**).

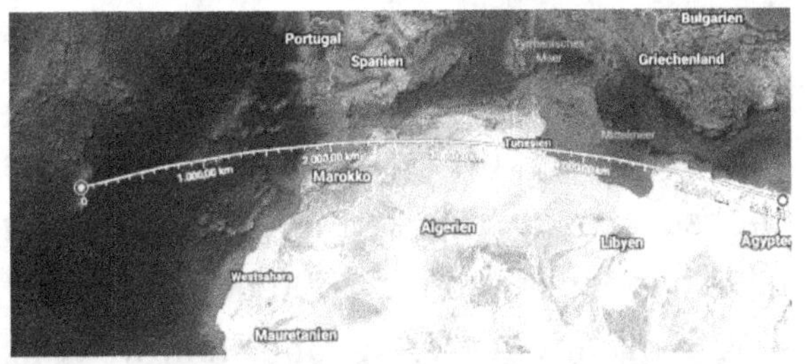

Fig.4: It is about 5638 km from the circular construction at the bottom of the atlantic ocean to the Great Sphinx in Egypt.

The great Sphinx in Giza keeps looking to the east, however he possibly came from the west, because the pyramids are behind him.

A sphinx per se is a creature that includes a mystery, which is to solved and can be solved.

Translated, sphinx nowadays means "that which receives life". The name already provides a clue for solving the mystery.

The Great Sphinx is exactly positioned and aligned on a straight line to the latitude 29°58′ N, which I already mentioned above.

Of course, one can assume that the positioning of the Great Sphinx is not random. Why did the ancient egyptians choose exactly this latitude, which must have happened around 2500 before Christ?

In any case, if one follows this latitude from the Great Sphinx towards the west, one first and directly encounters the middle pyramid (Chephren). In the further course you will meet the west coast of Africa.

The solution of the mystery of the Great Sphinx lies in the not accidental orientation (=latitude, look to the east and origin from west) as well as in its dimensions:

The Great Sphinx has a total of 20 toes, or fingers. The corresponding unit of the ancient egyptian is remen (= 20 digits). At this point I would like to refer to wikipedia, where a nice overview of the ancient units of the Egyptians can be found.

The dimensions of the sphinx are 27,5 Remen long and 7,5 Remen high. That corresponds to 73,5 meters length and 20,2 meters height.

Multiplied together the dimensions of the Great Sphinx give 207 Remen, which corresponds to 1470 meters. The length and the height, in addition to the orientation and positioning, are the dimensions carefully selected by the builders.

Equipped with this knowledge, we now go back to the west coast of africa, that is, to the point one arrives at after following the latitude of the Great Sphinx towards the West.

This is where the name of the sphinx comes into play. It means that he somehow gave life.

So we are now on the west coast of africa with a view of the atlantic.

It is not a magic thought to assume that just this coast at this point "has given life"., which means somebody must have arrived here safely.

So the origin of the meaning of the sphinx must lie further to the west, that is, where nowadays the water, the atlantic, lies.

If you walk from this point, which has given life, 1470 kilometers along the latitude, or 3 times 207 Remen (because of 3 pyramids), in the direction of the atlantic ... where do you get there?

Well, I cut it short: you get pretty much on the circle of the above-mentioned sunken island group (**Fig.5**).

Fig.5: Is it coincidence if one can reach the sunken islands starting at the Great Sphinx?

To hold on to it, or to tell the other way round: The Great Sphinx, with its position and orientation, means that we should follow its latitude towards west.

When we do that, we get to the coast, the rescuing shore, which literally is the sphinx.

Now let's use the sphinx itself and take its shape, we end up in a construction sunk in the Atlantic, which may lool like a former gigantic city.

Could it then be assumed at this point, that from this position to which the sphinx directed us, comes the people who built the sphinx to commemorate their origin?

Why should the sphinx guide us precisely to this point through its exact orientation, positioning and dimensions, if there should not be anything important there?

Following this deduction, it must have been the case that a kind of flood destroyed this city. If was not by chance that it was narrated by that Platon, and it must have happened at about 9000 before Christ.

That is undoubtedly true, as the sea level was about 120 meters lower, and nowadays all those islands are under water.

Such a catastrophe, like a deluge, can mean that some or even many people have been able to save themselves.

This could only have happened with boats, which allowed the shore (that what has given life) to be reached, i.e. the west coast

By the way, in front of the pyramids there are boat pits, where there is no shortage of explanatory possibilites, but in this context it must appear much more obvious what they are intenden for.

In the pictorial retelling of the destruction of their homeland, as much detail has been incorporated as is necessary to understand the story: The rescue by boats to the rescue shore, which ensured the survival.

For the last skeptic, of whom there are certainly more than those people who are fascinated, the following argument must be clear:

Not least, one must adhere to the only credible source that describes Atlantis and its localization.

If Platon in his report describes that Atlantis is beyond the Pillars of Atlas (also termed Pillars of Hercules), so does it.

The Pillars of Atlas are just about 2156 kilometers from the circular sunken city (**Fig.6**).

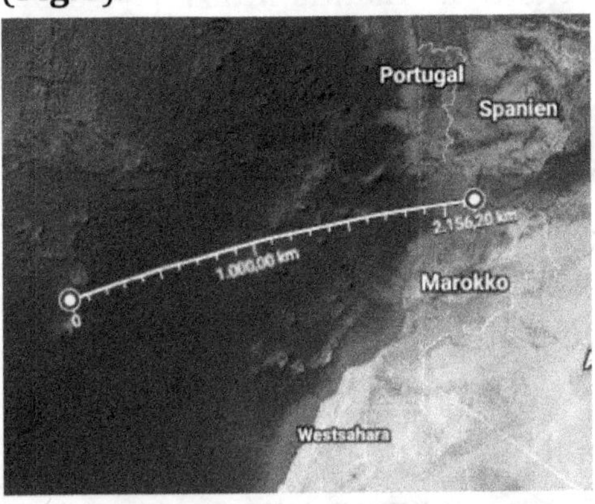

Fig.6: Distance from the Pillars of Atlas to the sunken city is about 2156 kilometers.

If one counts the archipelago, which at that time must have existed there (compare Fig.1), then the distance is even much shorter and thus almost in front of the house.

And Atlantis, due to Platon´s description, can not be located near Mexico, Brazil or even further away. As an example, who describes a baker on the other side of the street "it is straight there" but means a location elsewhere in another country?

In this respect, any skeptic should concede that Atlantis MUST (!) be beyond these pillars.

This eternal lament and foolish argue: Yes, because Atlantis is a myth, blablabla, ist does not exist, Platon told us a great story, doesn´t he, however, we assume Atlantis is there or there.

Common sense can not be completely suspended in such a way.

In summary, from my here and quite obvious explanations, I would therefore like to state:

1) In the northern Atlantic, south of the Azores, lie the remains of a gigantic circular complex. That is a hint on Atlantis.

2) This complex was still above water in 9000 before Christ, and was therefore inhabitated because the geometric objects can only be created by human hands.

3) This complex liest not far from the Pillars of Atlas, the place described by Platon as the localization of Atlantis.

4) It is not accidental that the former city is located on the exact latitude of the Great Sphinx, which, translated and interpreted, may represent a rescuing shore.

5) The reports about Atlantis come from ancient Egypt, and not coincidentally because Atlantis is the past of the ancient Egyptians.

Thus, the pyramid complex of the ancient Egyptians can and should be interpreted as a monumental replica of the geography and culture of Atlantis.

This momument has been telling the story of destruction and rescue for thousand of years, and will continue to do so.

The three pyramids symbolize, it may be assumed, three populations of Atlantis, or three of the inhabited plots of the gigantic island state.

In the disaster, these people were able to reach the rescuing shore, the west coast of africa. That explains with ease the existing boat pits east of the pyramids.

What is completely new and spectacular about this derivation is that the Egyptian culture obviously has something directly to do with the culture of Atlantis.

Whether the Egyptians descended from Atlantis, is for one or the other still an open question.

However, the work-up alone as well as the presentation as gigantic pyramids, a staging, an open-air stage, a drama, must require a very close relationship to Atlantis, which can only be explained by direct descendants.

I am pretty sure that there are many more direct correlations of arrangement and dimensions of the pyramids on Atlantis possible and available.

Therefore, the dimensions of the pyramids, and in particular their height, must have something to do with the people or islands of Atlantis in adescriptive manner.

Also, the geographic location of Atlantis itself or its islands should be recorded here in this spectacle.

At this point you may ask, what this is about. Why is there a giant circle on the ground of the atlantic ocean, the remains of a former city. What is or was its purpose?

To give you the answer, I would like to start with the triangle in the south of atlantis (**Fig.7**). It is equilateral, with a sidelength of 14 units each.

If you have not believed me so far, at the end of this derivation, you will.

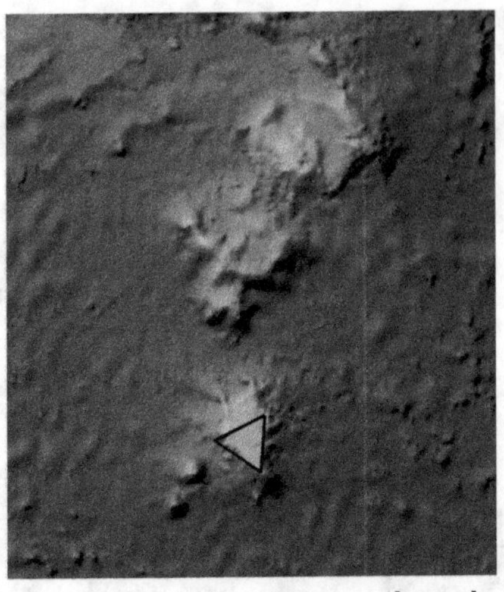

Fig.7: In the south of Atlantis an equilateral triangle (60 degrees angles inside) exists.

As a sidenote, an angle of 60 degrees is important for the Eye of Providence, also called the all-seeing eye of God. The ancient Egyptians may have adopted this template from Atlantis.

You can draw a line from the right side of this triangle towards north (**Fig.8**).

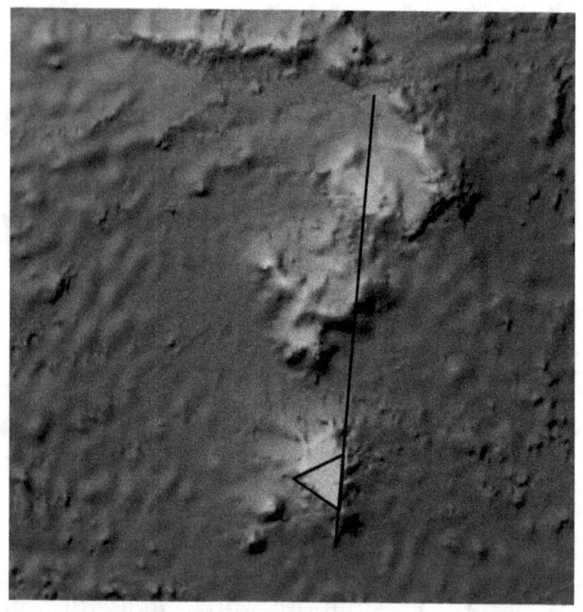

Fig.8: By elongation of the right side of the triangle, you can draw a line towards north.

At exatc 4 times elongation of the triangle´s side length (i.e. 4x14 Units), another triangle can be placed.

That is an exact copy of the first triangle, with same dimensions and orientation (**Fig.9**).

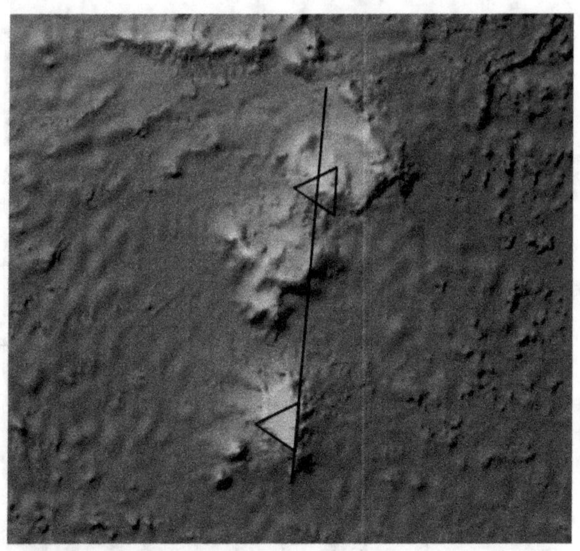

Fig.9: A second triangle can be placed at 4 times elongation of the side length.

The line moves straigth through the point of the triangle, from which you can draw the altitude of the triangle. In this case it is 12,12 Units.

The altitude accurately defines the radius of the circle, that can be seen there on the ground of the atlantic ocean (**fig. 10**).

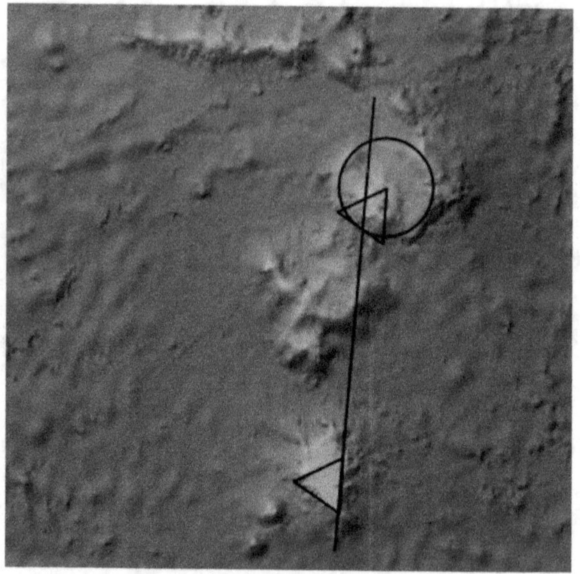

Fig.10: The attitude of the second triangle defines the radius of the circle that is visible on the ground.

So, we got now two geometric shapes of atlantis and have connected them. The first triangle is required to draw the circle, utilizing an exact copy of it.

The next step is to utilise the second triangle again. A line is drawn, moving through the centre of the circle as well as the point from which we draw the attitude of the triangle (**Fig.11**).

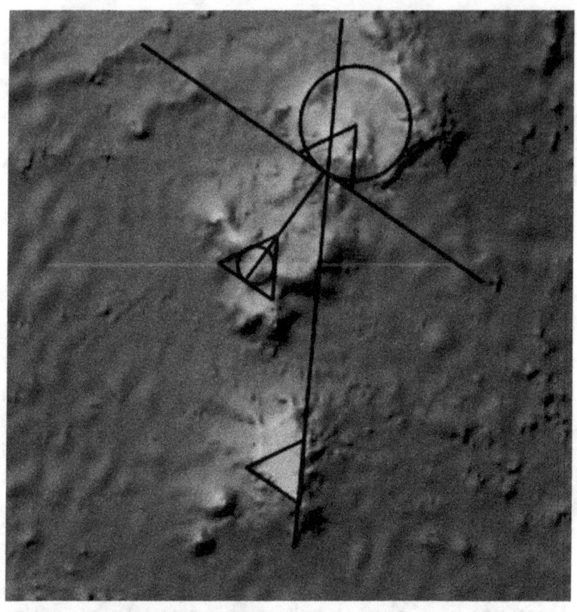

Fig. 11: A third triangle is placed in the centre of Atlantis, utilising the second triangle, at 2 times elongation of the sidelength (i.e. 28 Units).

You may have noted that this triangle marks the exact centre of Atlantis. In fact, we used the first triangle to construct two exact copies of it, and cover the first two landmarks of Atlantis: The small circle in the north, and the centre.

Now, tangents play an important role. We draw one alongside the side of the second triangle that touches the circle (**Fig.11**).

Simultaneously, in the third triangle the inner circle can be drawn. Using the centre of this inner circle, we put a line exactly in the direction of the tangent.

At the point that line hits the tangent, we receive two things:

First, a line that moves exactly from east to west, and second, the radius of the great circle (**Fig.12**).

It is amazing that, using the triangle in the south, the great circle can be drawn. You realize that both, the triangle and the great circle, and even the small circle, are structures that are actually there.

By placing the two additional triangles, the small circle as well as the centre of Atlantis are marked.

However, that is not the end yet, and we move on, because this is going to be exciting.

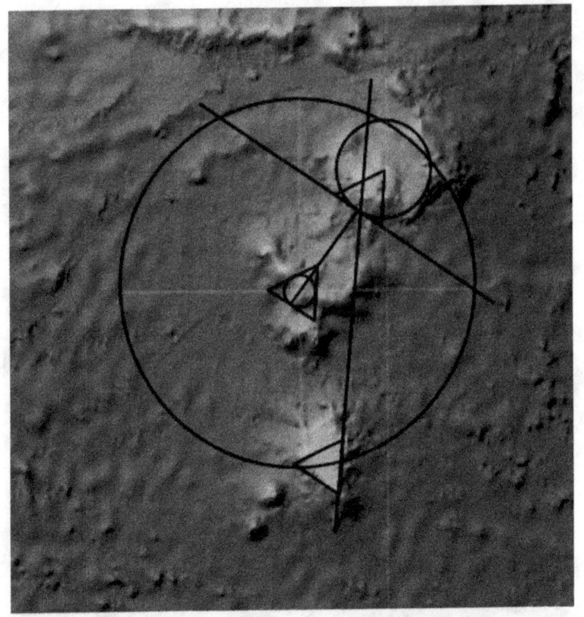

Fig.12: The great circle can be obtained by the steps
I present you here.

Is anyone still doubting, that the
formations on the ground of the atlantic
ocean are in fact Atlantis?

Well. For sure you may ask what a
giant circle has to do there, what is its
purpose?

To give you the answer, we draw a
second tangent using the third triangle
(**Fig.13**). In addition, I marked three

intercept points of the great circle and the two tangents, as well of the starting point.

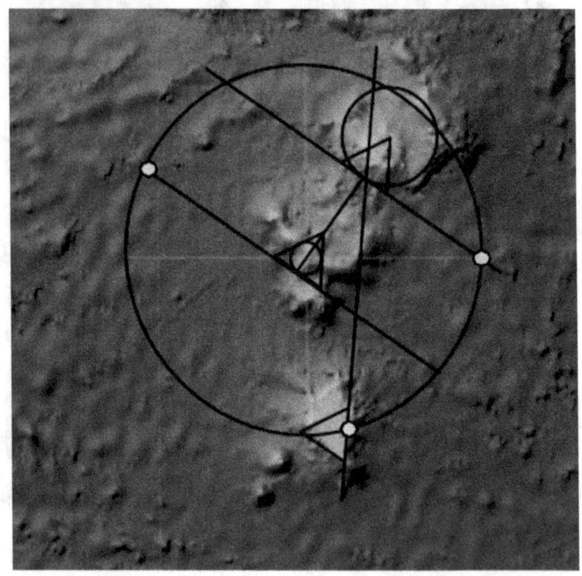

Fig.13: Here, three important intercept points are marked.

Now, give us a few moments and just let this picture work on you. In the meantime, we make a trip into the infinite vastness of the universe.

We are looking to the north, of course north! In the sky, we can see the following picture (**Fig.14**).

Fig.14: The so-called summer triangle is a constellation of three stars: Vega, Altair and Daneb.

Looks nice, doesnt it? But, and I do not know If anyone has recognized that before, did you know that the three stars of that constellation locate on a circle?

No? Same for me. So please have a look (**Fig.15**).

Fig.15: Amazing, isnt it?

Speaking of circles, we go back to Atlantis, because we have demonstrated that there is a giant circle surrounding the site.

Do you recognize something? Concerning the intercept points?

I will give you a hint: I copied the intercept points, rotated them together at around 160 degrees, and get the picture as shown (**Fig.16**).

Fig.16: The positions of the stars of the summer triangle are exactly the intercept points on the ground of the atlantic ocean.

You have to rotate the points simply because you require a distinct season and a specific date to match them. I chose a picture of any season.

That means that someone has to figure out which exact date is required to obtain the position of the three stars that is given by Atlantis. I guess it must have to do something with summer solstice.

Nevertheless, you may go one step further. The position of Altair defines the position of the two other stars, because they are connected.

That means, one can read that distinct position of the summer triangle constellation simply by using sundown.

If the sun goes down at the position of Altair, you receive a very specific date. And that is it: Atlantis is a giant and ancient calender, much older than stonehenge.

That is by far the greatest story I have ever heard. Is it a story? Or is it history?

The author
Dr. Michael Hoffmann

Hints:

Figures in this book are kindly provided by google, and are copyright material.

The rest of the derivation does not require a source specification, because it represents common knowledge and otherwise is created from my logical conclusions.

Parts and pre-Versions of this little book has been send to the Deutsche Gesellschaft für Ur- und Frühgeschichte e.V. and have been discussed on the Ärchaologie Forum Online, respectively.

In addition, a pre-Version was send to the journal Archäologie in Deutschland.

The purpose of these actions was to draw attention to discovery. Also, it should be excluded that these objects have already been discovered.

As far as I can say at this Point now: This discovery is incredibly cool!

And to give this matter some speculation here in this book:

According to Platon, a temple of Poseidon is said to have been located in the centre of atlantis.

A greek god of water, back and forth, also other cultures had their gods. Those who live surrounded by water also find a suitable god for this.

As depicted in Fig. 3, right in the centre of Atlantis, a strange hill formation localizes. Does it look like a trident? I guess not.

But I think, this is not a random ground shape, it must have a meaning. May be that shape knows a god?

Or, does it point to something in the north, or even at the sky?

It would be interesting to figure that out.

About the author:

Dr. Michael Hoffmann was born on 30.08.1973 in Düsseldorf, Germany. He studied biology and after his doctorate, he was researching rare diseases at the University´s Children Hospital.

From 2013, he had to freeze his scientific career for private reasons. Since then, he has occasionally published novels, little books, but also scientific articles.

Important is also on this booklet:

Do not take everything too seriously!

It is easy written, und it should be read easily. Certainly, there are millions of know-it-alls, and everyone has already discovered his Atlantis.

Anyway, a small overview of the author can be found on his website:

www.michaelhoffmann.org

For Daniela, in love.